A New True Book

MARSHES AND SWAMPS

By Lynn M. Stone

This "true book" was prepared
under the direction of
Illa Podendorf,
formerly with the Laboratory School,
University of Chicago

CHILDRENS PRESS ™

CHICAGO

Everglades

PHOTO CREDITS

Mark Rosenthal—2, 41, 43

James P. Rowan—4 (top), 23 (right), 35 (right)

Reinhard Brucker—4 (bottom), 17

Jerry Hennen—6, 9 (2 photos at top), 10 (right), 11 (right), 12 (4 photos), 14 (2 photos), 15, 18 (2 photos), 19 (right), 21 (3 photos), 23 (left), 29 (right), 31, 34, 36 (above right)

Lynn M. Stone—cover, 7, 9 (2 photos at bottom), 10 (left), 11 (left), 19 (left), 22 (left), 25 (top, bottom left and right), 26 (2 photos), 27, 28, 29 (left), 30, 32 (2 photos), 36 (above left, bottom left and right), 38, 40 (2 photos), 45

Kitty Kohout—16

Jerome Wyckoff—22 (right)

James Mejuto—25 (middle)

Bill Thomas—35 (left)

COVER—Big Cypress Swamp

Library of Congress Cataloging in Publication Data

Stone, Lynn M.
  Marshes and swamps.

  (A New true book)
  Summary: Describes the plants and animals that live in wetlands such as swamps, marshes, and bogs, and emphasizes the importance of wetlands to the earth's ecology.
  1. Wetland ecology—Juvenile literature. 2. Wetlands—Juvenile literature. [1. Wetland ecology.
2. Ecology. 3. Marshes. 4. Swamps. I. Title.
QH541.5.M3S76   574.5'26325   82-17861
ISBN 0-516-01681-4   AACR2

TABLE OF CONTENTS

Wetlands. . . 5

Marshes and Swamps Are Important. . . 8

Marshes. . . 16

Salt Marshes. . . 24

The Bog. . . 27

Swamps. . . 31

The Mangrove Swamp. . . 37

The Everglades. . . 41

Things to Remember. . . 44

Words You Should Know. . . 46

Index. . . 47

Cypress Swamp

Marsh in late fall

WETLANDS

You probably have swum in a pond or lake. You may have fished in one.

Most ponds and lakes are deep. Very few plants grow above the water. The plants grow along the edges or under the water.

Marshes and swamps are places that hold water, too. But marshes and swamps are not very deep.

Some marshes become swamps.

Marshes and swamps
have soft, muddy bottoms
where plants often take
root. Many of these plants
send their leaves, stems,
and flowers above the water.

Marshes come from
ponds. Dead plants in
ponds begin to pile up.

Big Cypress Swamp

They make a soil that
begins to fill the pond.

In time, marshes fill in,
too. When the marsh is
shallow enough, trees root
there, and then it is called
a swamp.

MARSHES AND SWAMPS ARE IMPORTANT

Some of the water we use in our homes is stored in marshes and swamps. Some of the fish and animals we eat grow up there. Many kinds of plants and animals live in these wetlands.

People use them to raise cranberries and rice. Some logs come from trees that grow in wetlands.

Above left: Fisher spider on pond lily
Above: Wild cranberries
Left: Green tree frog
Below: Woodpecker in palm

Look closely when you
visit a marsh or swamp.
You will see birds. You will
see insects. You might see
a frog, snake, or turtle.

Above: Muskrat
Left: Tiger salamander eating an
earthworm

In the spring, you might
see a salamander or toad.
You might even see a
beaver, mink, or muskrat.

Some of the animals you
see spend their entire lives
in the wetlands. Water
snakes and frogs rarely
leave.

Above: Canada geese
Left: Water snake with fish

Some other animals only visit. Geese may come just to rest on the water. A buffalo stops just for a drink or a mouthful of plants.

Top: Mallard duck
with ducklings
Above left: Duckweed
Above right: Doe deer
at edge of pond
Right: Wood duck

12

Many of the plants and animals of the wetlands are too small to see.

Still, these tiny plants and animals are very important to the life of the wetlands. They are food for larger animals.

Some animals eat plants. The muskrat and deer eat plants. Ducks eat marsh plants, such as the tiny green plants called duckweed.

Above: Dragonfly
Right: American toad

When you visit a marsh or swamp, listen. Did you hear the calls of birds, the croaks of frogs, or the buzzing sounds of dragonflies?

In the spring, listen for a loud, whistling sound. That is the sound made by a toad.

Winter in the northern wetlands

A winter visit will be a quiet time. Snow and ice cover the water. The marsh birds have flown south.

Many animals have crawled into the mud. There they can stay alive under the snow and ice until spring.

Cattails

MARSHES

Many kinds of plants grow in marshes. One is the cattail.

Cattails are tall plants with long, thin leaves. The top of each plant looks like a fuzzy cat's tail.

Muskrat
house

Marsh plants are very useful to animals. The muskrat eats cattail roots. Some marsh animals use cattails for their homes. Much of the muskrat's house is made of cattails.

Birds make nests of cattails. Some of these nests are made to float!

Above: Crayfish
Left: Raccoon

Raccoons hunt in marshes. They eat clams and crayfish.

Deer come to the marsh to drink and eat plants.

Tall birds with long legs and long, sharp beaks come to the marsh. They hunt frogs, fish, insects, and snakes. With their long legs, these birds can wade into the marsh water.

Ducks, geese, and swans fly to marshes to rest and eat. Some of them build nests in the marsh.

Right: Coot nest
Below: Mute swan

White pelicans fly to marshes to fish.

Red-winged blackbirds are the most common birds in the marsh. Yellow-headed blackbirds are common in some marshes.

Shorebirds hunt along the edges of the marsh. They hunt for tiny animals that live in the mud. The killdeer is a shorebird that calls its name: kill-deer, kill-deer!

Top: A killdeer pretends to be hurt
in order to lead an enemy
away from its nest. When
the enemy is far enough
away from the nest,
the killdeer flies away.
Left: Yellow-headed blackbird
Above: Red-winged blackbird nest

Above: Green frog
Right: Frog eggs

The marsh animals with soft, moist, smooth skin and four legs are called amphibians. They begin life in the water. As adults they can live on land or in the water.

Frogs, toads, and salamanders are amphibians.

Amphibians lay eggs in the marsh. Frog eggs look like a mass of jelly. Toad eggs look like a string of black dots.

Some marsh plants are colorful as well as useful.

Left: Marsh marigold
Right: Blue flag iris

SALT MARSHES

Marshes along the ocean have mostly ocean water in them. Ocean water is salty. These wetlands are called salt marshes.

Oysters and clams live in the mud of salt marshes. Fiddler crabs live here, too.

Blue crabs live in the salt marsh water. Herons and egrets also hunt in salt marshes.

Above: Salt marsh
Left: Close-up of salt marsh
    grasses that can live in
    salt water.
Below left: Egret
Below: Fiddler crabs have one
    big claw that they
    carry like a fiddle.

Above: White ibis hunting
Left: Great blue heron at its nest

The ibis has long legs like the herons, but it has a curved bill. The ibis uses its bill to find animals in the salt marsh mud.

Many wading birds build nests of salt marsh grass.

Leatherleaf bog. Plants often cover the water in a bog.

THE BOG

A bog is very much like a swamp or marsh. Sometimes a thick, strong blanket of plants grows over the water!

Walking on a bog blanket is like walking on

a mattress. Each step seems
to shake the whole bog.

Grasses, bushes, trees,
and moss grow in bogs.

Bogs often have a pond
in their center.

Many northern bogs have
tamarack trees.

Tamarack trees
have needle leaves
like Christmas
trees.

Pitcher plants (above) and sundew plants (left) catch insects.

Some very unusual flowers grow in bogs. The pitcher plant and sundew catch insects! Insects that crawl into a pitcher plant become trapped.

The sundew is sticky.
Insects sometimes become
caught on the sticky hairs.

Scientists think that
these insect-eating plants
actually use insects for
food.

The bog's prettiest
flowers are lady's slippers.

Showy
lady's slipper

Red maple

SWAMPS

Swamps are marshes with trees. Many different kinds of trees grow in swamps.

One tree is the red maple. Its leaves turn red each fall.

The cypress tree grows in swamps. Cypress trees

Views of a cypress swamp with a close-up of cypress knees (above)

have very thick trunks.
They also have parts
called knees.

The knees have strange,
twisted shapes. They grow
up around the trunk.

Cypress wood is very
valuable for building. It
almost never rots.

Swamps are homes for
several kinds of animals.
Woodpeckers, owls, and
wood ducks live in swamp
trees. Frogs, turtles, toads,

spiders, small fish, insects, and snakes live in the swamp.

In the Far North, even moose come to swamps. Moose are big deer. Male moose have big, flattened antlers. Moose eat swamp plants.

Male moose are called bulls.

Left: The water moccasin is a poisonous
snake
Above: American alligators

In the South, alligators
and water moccasins live
in swamps.

Most water snakes are
not dangerous. But the
water moccasin is
dangerous. It uses its
poison to kill the frogs and
fish that it eats.

Above left: Skunk cabbage
Above right: Cardinal flowers
Left: Swamp lilies
Above: Yellow water lily

Many flowers grow in a swamp.

The skunk cabbage blooms in early spring. It smells like a skunk when its leaves are broken.

THE MANGROVE SWAMP

Remember the salt marsh? It had wild grasses that grew in salt water.

The mangrove swamp has trees that can grow in salt water!

Mangroves are bushy trees. Their roots look like spider legs. These trees grow only in very warm places.

Mangrove swamp

Mangrove swamps are found in shallow water close to the ocean.

Sea animals such as oysters and fiddler crabs live in the mud of the mangrove swamp. Many kinds of fish live here, too.

Raccoons live in mangrove swamps. They climb among the twisted roots and reach into the water. They often catch oysters.

Many birds nest in mangrove swamps. They build large nests of sticks.

Many birds wade in the mangrove swamp water. Some have long, sharp beaks. Some have bills shaped like spoons! The flamingo's bill is curved.

Above: Roseate spoonbills
Right: American flamingo

Many of the little fish that escape the hunting birds grow up here. They leave the mangrove swamps and swim to the ocean.

THE EVERGLADES

The southern tip of
Florida is a huge wetland.
Much of this wetland is
called the Everglades.

The Everglades is
something like a giant
marsh. It has tall saw grass

growing in it. This plant has a sharp, cutting edge.

The Everglades is something like a swamp, too. Many trees are scattered here.

The Everglades is even something like a river. Beneath the trees and grass, water flows south from a giant lake.

The Everglades is often called "a river of grass."

Many marsh and swamp

animals live in this
wetland: otters, alligators,
turtles, wading birds,
snakes, and others. A few
big, wild cats called
Florida panthers live here.

The Everglades is
unusual. No other wetland
on earth is quite like it.

THINGS TO REMEMBER

Bogs, swamps, and marshes are wetlands. They have plants growing above the water.

Many kinds of plants and animals need wetlands to survive. When we fill wetlands with dirt, we destroy them. Many bogs, swamps, and marshes have already been destroyed.

Ducks in a swamp

Wetlands are important. We eat many of the plants and animals that come from wetlands. Some of our drinking water is stored in wetlands.

Plants, animals, and people need wetlands!

WORDS YOU SHOULD KNOW

amphibian(am • FIB • ee • yan) — a group of animals living the early part of their lives in water and that later can live in water or on land. Frogs, toads, and salamanders are amphibians

bog(BAWG) — a soft, wet area of land

marsh(MARSH) — an area of low, wetland; a filled in pond

rare(RAIR) — not very usual; uncommon

swamp(SWAHMP) — an area of soft, wetland full of mud; a filled in marsh

wade(WAID) — to walk in water

INDEX

alligators, 35, 43

amphibians, 22, 23

animals, 8-11, 13-15, 17, 18, 22, 23, 33-35, 38, 39, 43, 44, 45

beaver, 10

birds, 9, 11, 13-15, 17-20, 24, 26, 33, 39, 40, 43

blackbirds, 20

blue crabs, 24

bogs, 27-30, 44

buffalo, 11

bushes, 28

cats, wild, 43

cattails, 16, 17

clams, 18, 24

crabs, 24, 38

cranberries, 8

crayfish, 18

cypress trees, 31, 33

deer, 13, 18, 34

dragonflies, 14

ducks, 13, 19, 33

duckweed, 13

eggs, amphibians', 23

egrets, 24

Everglades, 41-43

fiddler crabs, 24, 38

fish, 8, 19, 34, 35, 38, 40

flamingos, 39

Florida, 41

Florida panthers, 43

flowers, 29, 30, 36

frogs, 9, 10, 14, 19, 22, 23, 33, 35

geese, 11, 19

grasses, 28, 37, 41

herons, 24

ibis, 26

insect-eating plants, 29, 30

insects, 9, 14, 19, 29, 30, 34

killdeer, 20

knees, of cypress trees, 33

lady's slippers, 30

lakes, 5

logs, 8

mangrove swamps, 37-40

mangrove trees, 37

maple trees, 31

marshes, 5-9, 16-26, 31, 37, 41, 44

mink, 10

moose, 34

moss, 28

muskrat, 10, 13, 17

nests, 17, 19, 26, 39

otters, 43

owls, 33

oysters, 24, 38, 39

panthers, 43

pelicans, 20

pitcher plant, 29

plants, 5, 6, 8, 11, 13, 16-18, 23,
   27-30, 34, 36, 41, 42, 44, 45
ponds, 5, 7, 28
raccoons, 18, 39
red maple trees, 31
red-winged blackbirds, 20
rice, 8
"river of grass," 42
salamanders, 10, 22
salt marshes, 24, 26, 37
saw grass, 41
shorebirds, 20
skunk cabbage, 36
snakes, 9, 10, 19, 34, 35, 43
spiders, 34
spring, 10, 14
sundew, 29, 30

swamps, 5-9, 31-40, 42, 44
swans, 19
tamarack trees, 28
toads, 10, 14, 22, 23, 33
trees, 7, 8, 28, 31, 33, 37, 42
turtles, 9, 33, 43
wading birds, 26, 43
water moccasins, 35
water snakes, 10
wetlands, 8, 10, 13, 24, 41, 43,
   44, 45
white pelicans, 20
wild cats, 43
winter, 15
wood ducks, 33
woodpeckers, 33
yellow-headed blackbirds, 20

About the Author

Lynn M. Stone was born and raised in Meriden, Connecticut. He received his undergraduate degree from Aurora College in Illinois and his master's degree from Northern Illinois University. Once a teacher in Sarasota, Florida, Mr. Stone currently teaches English to junior high school students in the West Aurora Public School system.

A free-lance wildlife photographer and journalist, Lynn has had his work appear in many publications including National Wildlife, Ranger Rick, Oceans, Country Gentleman, Animal Kingdom, *and* International Wildlife. *He has also contributed to Time-Life. National Geographic, Audubon Field Guide, and Hallmark Cards publications.*

Many of Lynn Stone's photographs have been used in the New True Books published by Childrens Press.